YOUR KNOWLEDGE HAS VALUE

AF153492

- We will publish your bachelor's and master's thesis, essays and papers

- Your own eBook and book - sold worldwide in all relevant shops

- Earn money with each sale

Upload your text at www.GRIN.com and publish for free

Aljona Atamaniuk

The terms "multicultural", "cross-cultural", "intercultural". Meaning, differences, area of using

GRIN Publishing

Imprint:

Copyright © 2014 GRIN Verlag GmbH
Print and binding: Books on Demand GmbH, Norderstedt Germany
ISBN: 978-3-656-85630-6

This book at GRIN:

http://www.grin.com/en/e-book/280911/the-terms-multicultural-cross-cultural-
intercultural-meaning

GRIN - Your knowledge has value

Since its foundation in 1998, GRIN has specialized in publishing academic texts by students, college teachers and other academics as e-book and printed book. The website www.grin.com is an ideal platform for presenting term papers, final papers, scientific essays, dissertations and specialist books.

Visit us on the internet:

http://www.grin.com/

http://www.facebook.com/grincom

http://www.twitter.com/grin_com

Assignment on the topic: "The terms "multicultural", "cross-cultural", intercultural". Meaning. Differences. Area of using."

All human beings have culture, no matter which their level of formal education or where they were born. The meanings of the terms "multicultural", "cross-cultural", intercultural" have already explained by many scientists, but in spite of this nowadays they are discussions about what this words actually mean, what differences between them and in which area is it using of this words appropriate.

Multiculturalism is often contrasted with the concepts of assimilations and has been described as a "salad bowl" or "cultural mosaic" or „mixed salad". It is not necessarily mean that each person from society belongs to different cultures. A lot of human beings speak more than one language, many of us share more than one culture with different groups of people we interact with. (Burgess, 2005 p.31) The people who live in border regions or in such countries as Australia, some part of the USA and South Africa, where immigrants from some counties built the culture, have different cultures, which they are used to respect. For example, you can be Russian, but when you come back to Ukraine you can be German. Another scientists say that multiculturalism is a society "at ease with the rich tapestry of human life and the desire amongst people to express their own identity in the manner they see fit." (Bloor, 2010, p. 272) This meaning is partly combined with the first meaning, but it emphasises the behaviour of individual in society. A common aspect of many policies is that they avoid presenting any specific ethnic, religious, or cultural community values as central. Multiculturality begins when some develop the ability to understand foreigners according to these foreigners' own standards. Multicultural ideology refers to "overall evaluation of the majority group addressing the degree to which they possess positive attitudes toward immigrants and cultural diversity". (See, 1998)

Cross culture is more than a one culture, this means that often cultures are compared or contrast. Cultural differences may be understood or acknowledged, but are also managed in a way that does not allow for individual or collective transformation. (The United Church of Canada, 2011)

Intercultural is highly involved in process of maintaining the link between individuality and culture. There are mutually reciprocal relationships among and between cultures. The focus is on relationship building (not survival), deep connections, interactions, mutual gifting, respect, and learning from one another. (The United Church of Canada, 2011)

These three terms have as commonalities as differences. *Cross-cultural is a* comparison of two or more cultures. But Intercultural Studies, for example, "focus on the interaction of two or more cultures and answer the main question of what happens when two or more cultures interact (at the interpersonal level, group-level or international level). "In practice, however, the terms are often used interchangeably and unsystematic. While "Interculturality" refers to the process and the dynamics of social life, is primarily referred to as "multiculturalism" a social organization structure of the coexistence of different cultures and social groups. (Mooney, 2011, p.13) The difference between intercultural and multicultural is that intercultural means that there is an interaction between two or more cultures; multicultural means that something pertains to or is represented by many different cultures. The difference is interaction versus representation.

These terms can be used in different areas of life as in general in culture as in education or business. Intercultural can belong to the team or communication between people from different countries. Intercultural competence means being able to be open to listen and communicate with people of different cultural backgrounds have knowledge of the backgrounds of cultural groups, knowledge of existing stereotypes and prejudices involving cultural groups.

The use of words "cross-cultural" and "multicultural" and "intercultural" can be noticed in international business and organisations because nowadays the success of firm depends upon the smooth of interaction of employees from different cultures and regions.

One of the most prominent areas in promoting multiculturalism is the field of education. Statistics showed that most hate crimes occurring in schools or colleges are related to racial bias, religious bias, and bias against victims' ethnicity or national origins. Therefore, teachers play an important role in helping students develop a multicultural perspective to appreciate cultural diversity and other perspectives. (Arizaga, 2005, p.136)

These terms can be generally used and described, belonging to word "organisation". A Multicultural Organization consists of a group of people who celebrate each other's cultural backgrounds and traditions but does not address deeper level interactions and relationships. A Cross-Cultural Organization reflects a group that moves beyond surface level relationships by sharing and learning from each other's cultural heritage. An Intercultural Organization builds deep relationships due to sharing, understanding, and respecting each other's unique cultural backgrounds.

My point of view is that the multicultural can be community, where all people with different cultures live alongside one another and value tolerance, cuisine, festivals, dress and related things to culture. But all culture's values are not deep learning by society.

Cross-cultural applies to something, which covers more than one culture. It means to find way and to build relationship between similar cultural communities. In this way some cultures can be crossed and due to sharing, learning some features of culture appears from two cultures one united culture.

The term „intercultural" means the deep connection between individuals and cultures. Respect, understanding, freedom, equality – all this words are related to word "intercultural". Intercultural Management is the cultural dimension, which influences the preferences, actions and interpretations of working people in various activities. Ignoring the cultural dimension can lead to critical incidents and intercultural conflicts.

Our class can be called in different ways: „Multicultural Management" or „Cross-cultural Communication". I guess that the majority of people who have never touched with terms "multicultural", "cross-cultural", intercultural", would suggest to call our seminar "Multicultural Management" because many people would claim that multi – it is the same as many. So, as many culture you learn, as more competence you have. But when we correctly define this three terms, it is clear that an appropriate name for course like this is "Intercultural Management". The main reason for choosing this adjective is that this course is made to teach us to be competent in interaction (the term "intercultural" implies also interaction) understanding, behaving, adoption to different cultures and to have developed skills to work in intercultural atmosphere.

Bibliography

1. Arizaga, M., Bauman, S., Waldo, M., & Castellanos, L. P. Multicultural sensitivity
    and interpersonal skills training for pre-service teachers. Journal of Humanistic
    Counselling, Education and Development, 2005, American Counselling Association,
    p. 208.

2. Bloor Kevin. The Definitive Guide to Political Ideologies. 2010, AuthorHouse, p. 332.

3. Burgess, Ann Carroll; Burgess, Tom. Guide to Western Canada (7th ed.). Globe
    Pequot Press. 2005, 320 p.

4. Mooney Anne-Marie Cotter. Culture clash: an international legal perspective on ethnic
    discrimination. Ashgate Publishing, Ltd., 2011, p. 388.

5. See Hart, William B.: "What is Intercultural relationship, The Edge: The E-Journal of
    Intercultural Relations, 1998.

6. The United Church of Canada, Defining Multicultural, Cross-cultural, and
    Intercultural, 2011.